A Father's Ruin

HARRY JONES

authorHOUSE

AuthorHouse™ UK
1663 Liberty Drive
Bloomington, IN 47403 USA
www.authorhouse.co.uk
Phone: 0800 047 8203 (Domestic TFN)
*   +44 1908 723714 (International)*

© 2019 Harry Jones. All rights reserved.

No part of this book may be reproduced, stored in a retrieval system, or transmitted by any means without the written permission of the author.

Published by AuthorHouse 06/07/2019

ISBN: 978-1-7283-8925-7 (sc)
ISBN: 978-1-7283-8926-4 (e)

Print information available on the last page.

Any people depicted in stock imagery provided by Getty Images are models, and such images are being used for illustrative purposes only.
Certain stock imagery © Getty Images.

This book is printed on acid-free paper.

Because of the dynamic nature of the Internet, any web addresses or links contained in this book may have changed since publication and may no longer be valid. The views expressed in this work are solely those of the author and do not necessarily reflect the views of the publisher, and the publisher hereby disclaims any responsibility for them.

Contents

Acknowledgements.. vii
Prologue.. ix

Chapter 1   The return 1
Chapter 2   Home coming... 9
Chapter 3   The beginning of the End........................ 13
Chapter 4   Hatred 19
Chapter 5   Pam 35
Chapter 6   Rabecca 44
Chapter 7   Move to Halifax...................................... 67
Chapter 8   On the rise... 73
Chapter 9   The full truth 75
Chapter 10   Help 78

Synopsis 81

Acknowledgements

Firstly, I would like to thank my children for always being my boys. Secondly, I would like to thank my dad. Thank you for your support and advice. We haven't always seen eye to eye throughout this, but you're my dad and I love you regardless, and I know you always had the best intentions throughout everything. I can't thank you enough.

If I can be half the father to my boys that my dad has been to me, I know I've done a good job. I will always be there, good or bad for my children, as my dad has for me and my three brothers.

I would also like to thank the NHS, you have been a rock to me, and when nobody else could help, my doctor, my psychiatrist and psychologists all helped me. They didn't judge me and turned my way of seeing things just by listening to me and helping me realise life is worth living, and I am not the only one I'm sure.

To the families and friends of comrades' past and present, gone but never forgotten.

Last but not least, for all of you who suffer, this one is for you.

Prologue

Thank you for reading this, by the end of this you will hopefully have a much better understanding of how PTSD can affect the lives of more than just the person who is suffering with it. I have been rock bottom, and right now, thanks to the remarkable NHS, and my family, my life is on the up. I have turned it around and it is possible.

There is help out there, if you are suffering, need help, know someone who might be suffering or just have an interest, then this book should help you to a much better understanding. I will explain a lot about my life, but please don't expect details of reasons for my suffering. I have changed names for the safety of others, and I have asked permission of some to have their names kept as they are. I will tell you some horrible things I have done, and how I have made things better, I have now got my act together after many years of suffering and doing some things I wouldn't dream of doing if I wasn't suffering. The outcome outweighs the years of suffering. I have made some mistakes, and I reaped what I sewn, but I understand now and I am a much better man now, a real man, with real views and beliefs. I urge you not to judge me, at least till you have walked a mile in my shoes. Once you have, then you have earned the right to judge me.

I am donating some of the proceeds from this book to Combat Stress, a charity which doesn't get the recognition it deserves, and if my donations and this book can help the life of one person, it has all been worth it.

Good luck and God bless you all.

CHAPTER 1

THE RETURN

Camp Bastion, Afghanistan

The excitement can't be contained, we're finally going home. I can't wait to get back and see my boys. After a long, hot gruelling tour in Afghanistan, it'll be great to get back to normality. We were the OCC team in Nad' Ali, Helmand province. We were getting set to return back to Germany, before going on post tour leave.

"Gents, bad news I'm afraid" said the boss

"What's happened now Sir?" asked Phil

"Flights been delayed, the alarm that sounded 20 minutes ago was due to someone stealing a 4x4 and driving it on the runway. He was a local worker, and is now being questioned by the military police. We are lucky nobody was hurt but it is believed he was attempting to ram into one of the aircraft."

"Ungrateful twat" I said "he's given a job and does something like this, does he not realise we don't want to be here as much as he doesn't want us here? Fucking wanker"

"Harry, I know, but the flight is only delayed by 24 hours, so your flight will be in two days"

"That's not too bad I suppose" Said Andy.

"Naa, one more day won't hurt" I replied.

The boss then left the tent and headed back to his accommodation. We went to our welfare tent, there was nothing else to do so we watched BFBS on TV. An hour or so later, after a few brews I decided to go lay on my bed and read. I grabbed a book from the welfare tent and lay down. Unfortunately for us there isn't much fun things to do, people back home don't understand we have 1 channel, on 1 TV, which is shared by up to 400 soldiers at a time. We have books, most of which are boring and we can get magazines sent out to us, but the posties at the airport tend to lose them so they never arrive. We all know they end up at in their own bed spaces for their own personal use. Shocking I know, but it's a reality we have come to live with, and to be fair, anybody would do the same if they could get away with it.

Scoff time, we get our kit on and head off to the cook house. The food is shit, but it's better than starving, and I must admit, the military chefs do a difficult job, turning nothing into a little bit of something in a working kitchen in the desert. Could you imagine the heat? Scoff done, off to get a coffee at the café. A café might sound a bit posh, but it's a hut that you can buy a coffee from, it's pretty much the only luxury we get, and its only at the main camp, i.e. Camp Bastion. At the outposts there is nothing but rations. Back to the tent after coffee and start sorting my kit out ready to hand in the following day. Rifle cleaned, magazines cleaned, ammunition sorted, medical kit sorted, pistol cleaned, bayonet cleaned, and all ready to go. Bed time.

A Father's Ruin

The following morning, we all arose with a spring in our step, knowing that it was just a few hours till we were on the plane getting out of this hell hole. We went to see the CQMS to get our stuff handed in. We were to be without ammunition etc for 24 hours as the CQMS wasn't available the following day. It didn't matter though, there was enough armed personnel on the camp, it was the size of Reading after all. Time to go and spend the last of our dollars on coffee. We spent a few hours chatting, laughing and joking at the coffee house before heading back to our accommodation to ensure all our kit was packed and ready to go the next day.

Early bedtime but the excitement was too much to sleep. The darkness, whirring of helicopter rotary blades, the sound of armoured vehicles driving past was a sound I thought I wouldn't miss. I had been falling asleep to it for over six months now, never a silent moment. To go without the constant sweating in the blistering heat of the desert was exciting, and to actually smell clean for longer than 20 minutes was even more so. It may seem like nothing to most people but to us it was everything. People take for granted the little things in life, believe me, the little things are what make life worthwhile. To have a shower, and not sweat the moment you step out of it, to not have flies flying around you constantly, to not see rats running over your mosquito net through the night are all what we were looking forward too. That and a decent home cooked meal, a hug and kiss from our wives, girlfriends or partners, and to hold the hand of our children again was everything. I only hope that those of you who have never had to endure any of the things I have had too, never have to go through it.

Eventually we fell asleep, once we awoke in the morning it was shower and breakfast, then get our kit together. The CQMS took our bags to the airstrip for us; we followed and checked them in. Once our luggage was checked in, we then had hours to wait. As always, hurry up and wait. So, we decided to head off to get coffee and some lunch, off we went. Time was dragging; it always seemed to when the excitement was high.

Eventually it was time, our passports in hand; we went to the airstrip and got ourselves checked in. A bag of food was handed to us, and water was always on hand. A few beds were set out, this obviously meant our flight was going to be quite a wait, never have I caught an RAF flight that was on time. We tried to chill out, but all of us were on edge, just dying to get on the plane. Three hours passed, finally the air crew were ready. We moved through to another area, thinking we were going to board, turns out, we had to wait another hour before our flight. This couldn't get any more annoying, we saw the funny side though. After we waited, we went through a doorway where there was a lot of coaches waiting for us, we filled them, and headed to the plane.

We got off the coach to see the Hercules waiting on the runway with its tail down. We queued ready for boarding and slowly made our way onto the Hercules. The plane was full, the baggage was loaded, and the aircrew gave the safety brief. Ear protection was given out, and the engines were started. The plane was so loud it hurt your ears without ear protection. Even with ear protection you couldn't even hold a conversation with the person next to you because you couldn't hear a thing. So, we all sat in absolute silence, a whole three-hour flight to Cyprus unable to hear, unable to talk.

A Father's Ruin

We landed in Cyprus; we were taken to a camp to de-acclimatize. Due to the nature of work in Afghanistan we had to unwind. We were taken for food, and then shown to our accommodation for the night. Up early we were taken to the beach to have what we called forced fun; we were forced to join in with volleyball among other things. We spent the whole day there, six hours of which, most of us spent inside a building, sitting and waiting for the coaches to come back to take us to our accommodation. Finally, the coaches arrived and we all boarded. We were taken for some food, and we were handed some tokens for two beers that night. There was a CSE show put on for us at the camp, and we were allowed two beers. In all honesty, I had one beer and I went to bed. I just wanted to get home and see my wife and children. My youngest Tom was born just two weeks before I flew out to Afghanistan. My oldest, Luke, was only 3 years old and I had missed so much.

The following morning we awoke early, got ready, had breakfast and headed to the coaches to get us to the airstrip. We filled the coaches and headed off. This wasn't going to be our last journey, but we will get there eventually. We pulled up at the airstrip, passports in hand and headed to the check in desk. Got ourselves checked in, and went through to the waiting room. We found a comfortable spot as the wait was another three hours, and lay down. Three hours later we went through to the Boeing and boarded. The flight was headed to Brize Norton, and then our next flight was the following day. 5 or 6 hours later the plane landed in Brize Norton and we showed our passports. We headed off to our accommodation whilst everyone else had their loved ones there waiting to greet them. We slept through most of the next day and Jay, Keiron and I headed off to a local pizza place to have something which was different to what we'd been eating for months. It tasted amazing, we went back to the accommodation and we slept through the night.

The plane was ready, we were ready, let's get going. We checked in, and went through. We only had to wait two hours for this flight. We boarded and waited in excitement to take off on our 90-minute flight to Paderborn airport. Finally, we landed, grabbed our kit and went out. There was a minibus waiting for us, Mo was driving, he helped us load our kit onto the minibus and we got on the 30-minute drive to camp.

As we entered the gates of camp the pipes were playing, D squadron had a table with beer out the front of the offices and we were able to help ourselves. Before we did, everybody welcomed us back, and we began unloading the minibus.

"Daddy, would you like some help?" I heard from behind me. I turned around and there was Luke, my eldest, the smile it brought to my face was huge, behind him was my wife, Lucy and Tom. What a surprise, it was amazing. I picked up Luke, gave him the biggest hug and kiss, went over to Lucy, gave her a big hug and kiss and gave Tom a big hug and kiss. How I had missed them. It was the best surprise a man could ask for. She had contacted Captain Davies, the unit welfare officer and had arranged to book the welfare flat for two weeks whilst we had to do our two-week decompression. I went and thanked him for his help.

Once my kit was sorted, I jumped in the car and we headed to the welfare flat. We got in and I couldn't keep my hands off her. Once Tom had fallen asleep, Luke was watching TV and Lucy was cooking dinner I went into the kitchen. My hands began to wonder as I kissed her. She pulled me closer as she leaned against the kitchen wall. She undid my belt and pulled my jeans down to my knees, as she kissed me and took me in her hand, I undid her jeans and let them slip down. I pushed myself deep inside her, and it didn't take long for me to finish, but we both embraced each other as I did. We got ourselves sorted, had dinner and got the kids ready for bed. Lucy and I had a few drinks together, and held each other, naked throughout the night, she was so beautiful.

The following day, we headed off to the NAAFI for some breakfast. Luke was doing what children do and whinging about the food. Lucy shouted at him and stormed off to the toilet.

"Listen mate, please, just eat the food you've been given, be grateful for it, your Mum has had a lot of stress the last few months and you need to start doing as your asked. We wouldn't give you anything that's bad for you, would we?"

"No" he replied

"Right then, when you mum comes back, just say sorry and eat what's in front of you, ok?"

"Yes daddy"

She returned with a face like thunder, Tom in her arms.

"Sorry mummy" Luke said.

"It's ok darlin'" she responded.

So glad that was calmed down. We headed off to the shop to get some food in, then went back to the flat. I think we both needed a chill out. We put the TV on and cuddled together on the sofa.

The following day I had to go to work as usual, we had nothing to do, so we spent the day at the NAAFI on camp, doing nothing then lunch and early finish. This went on for the two weeks. We then jumped in the car, and drove to Rotterdam, got on the overnight ferry to Hull, then headed home. We got through the front door, at last, I'm home. Thank God for that. I sorted my kit out, and gave my family a hug. I sat on my sofa with a decent cup of coffee and watched more than one TV channel. Life was great, or so I thought................

Chapter 2

HOME COMING

Halifax, England

Four weeks leave; this is going to be bliss, so happy. We got up on the Saturday morning, had a coffee and decided to go out for the day. Somehow things didn't seem right, the mood was different, I felt different. It was the lack of sleep I thought to myself; we hadn't slept properly, the both of us. We went about our day, took the kids to the park, and then went shopping at the Trafford centre. I was due to start a course I had booked on the Monday. I wanted to do my close protection licence as a fall back, an extra qualification in case I decided to leave the Army. So it was great to spend this weekend together. The Monday came and I was off to do my CP course. It was residential, so another two weeks away, but I was hopeful it would be worth it in the long run. I couldn't have asked for a more supportive wife to put up with me being away so much.

During the course I received a phone call from my regimental Careers Management Officer.

"Corporal Jones, I have some good news for you"

"Oh Sir, what would that be then?"

"How would you like a posting to the AFCO in Worcester as a recruiter?"

"Sir, that'd be great, thank you"

"Right Corporal Jones, your course is booked ready, you will receive details on your return to unit, your posting will begin two weeks before the course and you will have a week's leave prior to the beginning of your posting. Is that ok for you?"

"Sir that's great news, thank you"

As soon as the phone call was over, I called Lucy to give her the good news. She didn't seem very impressed, so I put it down to stress and the fact that she was missing me. The course was over and I got myself home as quickly as possible. I couldn't wait to get home. I was home in three hours and was so happy. There was an atmosphere, but nothing we couldn't handle.

We went away for a few days, to stay in a caravan, it was lovely to relax, rest and recuperate.

Two weeks later I was on a flight back to Germany, not for long though, hopefully. I went to my room and unpacked. The following day I went on first parade, then went to Regimental headquarters to see the RCMO. I marched in and received my orders for recruiting. I went to the Quatermasters department and got MFO boxes ready to pack up my room and send it to Worcester. In three weeks I was posted.

A Father's Ruin

My kit all packed up and ready to send, I carried it all to the QM's department to be sent. It was only about six boxes of kit. Some of which I gave away as it was spares. So, back on leave, Glad to be back with my family, although something just didn't seem right, I wasn't sure if it was me or if it was Lucy, but we began arguing quite a lot. We were going to get a family portrait done one day, we had it all booked. On the way there, with the kids in the back of the car, an argument between Lucy and I broke out, I didn't know why, turns out neither did she, this wasn't good. From nowhere I heard "Can you please stop arguing" from Luke. That will haunt me for the rest of my life. I can't believe I upset my child that much at the age of 3 that he shouted at both his mum and I, and, he was right.

After the week was up, I went to Worcester. I had to stay at someone else's place until my accommodation was sorted but needs must. I walked into the office and introduced myself to everyone. They were a good bunch I was going to be working with, plus I was in the UK. That weekend I went back to Halifax, to see my family, the arguments continued. They became constant. I was offered work on a pub as a bouncer, to earn a little extra cash, I took it. It was an extra bit of money for us. I thought I would be doing the right thing in providing for my family, I was doing my best. Lucy and I kissed and made up and we were trying to get back to normal, but I was beginning to forget what normal was.

Back to work, then I was sent on my recruiting course. I drove to Bovington, Dorset where I was to do my course. It was a two-week course in which there was a lot to take in. I called Lucy every night, even then, on the phone we still argued. I was very unhappy, I felt alone, miserable and that my life was coming to an end.

Out of the blue I got a message on social media from a very old friend, we became friends and we were talking and getting on. I now realise I should never have started conversing with her; this was the beginning of the end.

Chapter 3

THE BEGINNING OF THE END

I had been waiting for three weeks for my accommodation and didn't want to keep putting people out, I called my brother, Jonathon and asked if it was ok for me to borrow his sofa until my flat was ready, he didn't mind. Plus, it was good to spend time with him. I went back home on the first weekend, and I was getting ready to go out to work. Lucy wanted to go to the bingo, I didn't start until the bingo had finished, so off she went. I was all ready for work when she came back.

"I think we need to talk" She said to me

"Ok babe, what about?"

"Are you having an affair?" she asked me. I was fuming that she could even think such a thing, never had I done anything like that to her.

"No, I'm fucking not, how dare you even think such a thing, where has this come from? Tell you what, fuck this,

I'm going to work" So off to work I went. It ran through my head all night, whilst working. I was convinced it was now over.

The pub closed and I walked home. As I walked in she was there with a cup of coffee ready for me. "We do need to talk" I said to Lucy.

"Ok, you first" she said.

"I can't keep going like this, I think we are over" I said as my heart sank into my stomach. The tears began to roll down her face, I couldn't believe I had done this to her, upset her so much. I was miserable though.

"I don't want it to end" she said.

"But I am extremely unhappy and have been for a while, can we fix it?" I asked her.

"Let's try?" She asked.

"Your right, we can't throw it all away, let's try again" I said.

That night we had the best sex I think we'd had throughout our marriage; it was amazing. The next morning, we got up and had a good day together. On the Sunday evening I drove to my brothers place and it was good, I felt good. My friend, Pam, messaged me asking how I was, I was honest, I'm good. She invited me over for coffee, I didn't see the harm in it, and so I went for a coffee. I now realise this was a huge error on my behalf.

Lucy and I continued on our downward spiral through the week and I had nobody to talk to about it. I started to talk to Pam about it, seeking advice and help; I was given more than I bargained for.

I never did the dirty; I didn't do anything with her. I was shown affection, support and I liked it. It was nice to be given some attention and the help I thought I needed, when in fact I was wrong, as I was to find out later on.

When I finished my course, my accommodation was sorted out, I invited Lucy to come and stay for a few days, in the hope that things could be sorted out. We were like different people, I was upset that this was how we were now, and I knew we were at the end. So, the following weekend, I went to home, and explained things.

"I'm very unhappy Lucy, I want to know if we can be fixed" I told her.

"Well you have a choice, go or stay" she said, the problem was, she said it with no kind of compassion, just with what appeared to be anger. She did nothing to show me she wanted to fix us, nothing to show she loved me and wanted it to work. After a few hours I had made the decision to leave. I sat with the kids on my lap, tears running down my face.

"Boys, I love you both more than anything in the world, I will always be here for you but I have to go. I'm not happy with Mummy, so I think it is better that we break up" I explained to them.

"But why Daddy" Luke asked me. This broke my heart, it broke me, I gave them the biggest hug, as the tears ran down my cheeks.

"This will not change how I feel about you boys and I want to see you as often as I can, I love you boys" I tried to re assure them.

I went upstairs and started to get my things together. Lucy came up and made the boys watch as I packed. I hated this and thought it was wrong. Maybe it was, maybe it wasn't but still, it was soul destroying.

Lucy sat on the bottom of the steps as I was about to walk out, I asked her "can this be fixed?"

"I don't know" was her reply

"Then I have to go" I said, I gave her a hug and walked to the car. I put my stuff in the boot, got into the driver's seat and I burst into tears. I picked up my phone and called my Dad.

"Hi son, you ok?"

"Dad, it's me and Lucy" I replied.

"What's happened son?" He asked with compassion.

"I've left her dad; I was unhappy and had to go" I explained.

"Oh son, I just want to give you a big hug, what are you going to do" he asked.

"I'm going to go to the flat in Worcester" I told him.

"Drive safe and call me when you get there" he asked of me.

"I will dad, speak to you soon".

I stayed sat in the car for about another hour, contemplating whether or not to go back in the house, trying to work out if I was making the right decision. I would find out the answer to that later.

I drove to Worcester, unpacked my stuff from the car, called my dad and lay on my bed. I was lost; I didn't know what to do. I couldn't sleep, hadn't eaten, I didn't want to eat. I text Pam for somebody to talk to, I told her everything and we talked for hours.

A few days later, she invited me for a drink, so I went, I had a good evening, it felt good, it was nice to relax. She kissed me, and I allowed it. It felt nice.

A Father's Ruin

The following day Pam told me it was a mistake; she said she shouldn't have done it. My life was topsy turvey and I didn't know where to go or what to do. I then began thinking I had made a terrible mistake and should never have left Lucy. I called my dad for advice. "Do me a favour Son, call her and tell her" he told me. I took his advice and I did just that. That weekend I went up to Halifax to see my children. I told Lucy to her face I thought I had made a mistake and I wanted her back.

"Really, well I don't think I want you back, and if I decide to you have some making up to do"

I thought that's it, we are over, I don't want to spend my life making up for one mistake, and I certainly don't need too. I'm human, I make mistakes, at least I had the balls to admit it. So, I left the house knowing that was it.

Pam called me a couple of days later and invited me for coffee, so I went. Again, we kissed, only this time she didn't say it was a mistake the following day. She text, me as normal, and it was nice. We continued to chat, and on the odd occasion we met for a drink or hot beverage and it was good. We decided after a couple of months to give a relationship a go.

I had to inform Lucy of this, but I didn't know the right time to do so. She then decided to tell me she wanted me back, so I did the honest thing and I told her I had met someone. She went berserk. She turned into a monster. My honesty had dropped me into huge trouble; I was in a hole and couldn't get out. I told Pam I had told her, she started receiving messages on social media, abusive messages, as did I. My name was dragged through the mud on social media and it was uncalled for. I was called every name under the sun and there was nothing I could do about it.

Eventually, things were calmed down, and Lucy and I talked. We agreed that the boys weren't to meet Pam yet, so I didn't allow it. A few months down the line things changed.

She threatened me with going to the child support agency (CSA), I offered her £1000 a month to ensure her and the kids had a roof over their heads and food on the table. She refused it and went to the CSA. I received a phone call informing me I had to pay a quarter of what I offered to her in child support. I text Lucy to tell her. I was disgusted by the response;

"Well played" was the response.

"Well played? This is my children, not a game, I made you an offer, not to play games, your greed got the better of you and this is what's happened, you chose this" was my reply. Funnily enough I got no response to that.

Chapter 4

HATRED

After a few months of seeing Pam I decided it was time to introduce my children. We went around to her house for a barbeque and the boys were introduced to Pam as my friend, not my girlfriend, to take things slow. I took the boys back to their house on the Sunday, she didn't greet them at the door and stayed sat on the sofa. On this journey my brother Jonathon agreed to come with me to keep me company. He went in the house and stood in the lounge as I sorted the push chair by the front door. Luke went into the lounge and was asked "did you have a good time?"

"Yeah, we met Daddies friend" He replied.

"Did you? Who was that?" She asked him.

"Pam" before Luke could get another word out, she was at the door shouting at me. She trapped me behind the front door yelling for me to get out. I went to walk out and she punched me from behind in the chin then kicked my legs. I stepped out and said "well that wasn't very clever was it"

"Do you want some more?" she stormed toward me.

"No thanks" I calmly said as I walked away. I have never and will never raise my hands to a woman. I refuse to, even when getting attacked as I did, I will not hit a woman. Jonathon and I got in the car and called my dad to source advice. We decided to go to the police when near where Jonathon lives. The journey was spent mostly in silence, both shocked that she had done this. We walked into the police station and both gave statements. Lucy was arrested the next day. I filed for divorce with my solicitor, which she refused to sign and things were not going right for me at all, even with Pam.

The police officers had the gall to say that I should man up and get on with it, but they have to arrest her. Once I had heard this, I called them to put in a complaint. I'm not being funny, but nobody deserves to be assaulted, whether it's by a man or a woman and should not be made to feel weak for reporting it. As far as I am aware, the officers involved with this incident were disciplined for their behaviour.

Now that the police were involved in all this, it was a tidal wave of abuse. I reported it, and they took a harassment order against her. This was my next mistake; I was unable to see my children. She not only stopped it, but so did the police because of harassment.

Pam had been messaging another man, telling him she wanted to be with him but couldn't leave me yet, I confronted her about it, and I was stupid enough to take her back, this was another mistake. Pam and I slept together for the first time, and it felt great. A few weeks later she informed me she was pregnant. I begged her to keep it, I would take care of the child and I would be there for it. She aborted, and it broke my heart. I swore from that day

A Father's Ruin

I would never, ever go through such a thing again, so I booked myself in for a vasectomy.

Shortly after this I was posted to Brighton careers office as the office manager. I was moved into a flat on the marina, I loved it, I wanted to stay there. On the weekends I would head back up to Birmingham to see Pam. We were getting on great. My divorce came through after a year of waiting, and I still hadn't seen my children throughout that year. Whilst I was unable to see my children, I did the only thing I could do and I wrote to them every week, without fail. I promised them in my letters that I would see them again, and I hoped that this was a promise I wasn't going to break.

After a few weeks of officially being divorced, I was offered work every other weekend at the biggest club in Brighton as a door man, I took it as it was work and paid my fuel for the weeks I travelled.

I was at my flat one evening and I received a text from Lucy;

"Hi, can I have your address please; Luke has drawn a picture for you and wants to send it". Without thinking I sent my address across, I was so excited about receiving something from my children. I waited in anticipation for this picture, only, two days later I received a letter ordering me to court in regards to the children. I read it carefully and the following day I printed off the same court application, filled it out and sent it to the courts in Brighton. I paid the money to the courts to have it implemented. Lucy was not impressed, but there was no way was I going to go without seeing my children. I wanted this issue sorting amicably and away from court, however, she chose this route, so I was going to fight with every ounce of energy I had for my children.

In the interim, to her applause, she agreed that I could see them every other weekend, so I would drive all the way up to Halifax on a Friday to pick them up, take them to Birmingham and do the return Journey on a Sunday. Pam didn't like it, but it was tough, my children came first.

Pam and I broke up often and repeatedly got back together, I met someone else whilst in Brighton, she was amazing, but we only hooked up whenever I was single. She made me feel good about myself, she was understanding and loving. Her name I will not mention in this book, as I don't feel it would be right to do so. We lost contact later on, so I also believe it would be irrelevant to talk on about her any further.

I went out one day and bought a ring, I knew Pam would like it, why I did it I don't know to this day, and I wish I didn't. On the weekend I went to Birmingham and that night I proposed to her. She said yes. Not once did I stop to think of what we had been through and what was more than likely going to happen. In all honesty, I knew at this stage that my head was all over the place and that I wasn't thinking straight.

At night I wasn't sleeping properly, the lack of sleep was affecting me. I was having nightmares when I did sleep, I began sleep walking at times and I was extremely unhappy with life as a whole. I went to see a doctor and tried to talk, but the doctor told me there was nothing wrong and I was fine, just a case of mild depression. This was a military doctor, and they were supposed to spot things that will come out later on. I decided to go elsewhere for the help I thought I needed, so I went to a walk-in centre in the hope they could help me. They told me to go and see my doctor, and I gave up trying to get help.

I was beginning to see things, things that I know weren't there, I was jumpy, hyper-vigilant, I was spotting vulnerable areas and points, I was believing there were snipers on roof tops watching me. My paranoia was immense. Bonfire night was an absolute nightmare for me, and still is to this day, and I believe it will be for the rest of my life.

I was given my court date for the children; I went to court in Halifax. I was nervous. I walked in and she had legal representation, I didn't. First thing she did was apologise for the assault that she was arrested and found guilty for, I accepted the apology. Following this, her solicitor did all the talking and I just listened. The session finished and we were given another date to return. This date was a month later. The following month I was there, Lucy had a different solicitor, she approached me;

"Mr. Jones can I have a word please" her solicitor asked.

"Certainly, in regards to what?" I responded.

"Lucy would like to come to an agreement" she informed me

"Ok let's talk" I said as I stood up, we went into a private room and she attempted to tell me what I was going to agree too. I very quickly stood my ground and declined all offers on the table. We went into court and this time it was my turn to shine. I explained my situation, I explained to the court that I was a dad that just wanted to see his children and be a father. I explained how she was preventing this from happening and she was attempting to dictate to me what I can and can't do with my children. Her solicitor stated at the end of the session that she will no longer represent Lucy, win for me.

I was given an appointment with Cafcass. I understood why, and that they were independent. The man with whom I had the appointment was friendly and honest. He informed me he had met with the children in school, and he had met with Lucy. We spoke and I was brutally honest with him. Realising this gentleman was not a liar in any way I asked him a question;

"Tell me, is what Lucy is doing to the children a form of metal abuse?" I asked him. He paused;

"Unfortunately, Mr. Jones, yes it can be seen as a form of mental abuse".

"Thank you, that's all I needed to know". The interview was over and we were done, I walked out with my head held high and was extremely proud of myself.

Another month passed, I was back in court, this time I had my dad and brother Jonathon with me in case I could call them in as witnesses. Once again she had a different solicitor, he approached me;

"Mr. Jones can we have a chat?" he asked.

"Certainly" I replied, I already knew he was going to try to avoid going into the court room. He made me an offer and I refused it;

"My counter offer is, I want to see my children every other weekend for two nights, plus I want them to be with me for half of the school holidays. Also in regards to Christmas, I would like to alternate Christmas day every year" I told him. He left the room to speak to Lucy; I knew the answer before he came back;

"She said no" he informed me. I told him I wouldn't change my mind, it's what I am going for as a minimum and I don't believe for one second it is unreasonable.

We entered the court room and sat in front of the magistrates. The legal assistant informed the Magistrates to be aware that I have no legal representation and could they take this into consideration. The Magistrates agreed. We moved on to our opening statements, I agreed for Lucy's Solicitor to go first. He did and it seemed he attempted to say she had offered me access which I had refused. It was my turn;

"Your Worships, I am a man, and a father, my children deserve to see their dad, to have a good role model in their lives. I am certain the children involved miss their father as much as I miss them. Is it a crime to ask for access to the children? I am a good, law abiding man, who works hard and would set a good example to my children. I am forced into the position to have to come to court because spite and hatred have overcome the emotional feelings toward the children from Ms. Jones. As much as she hates me, this should not prevent the children from having a relationship with their father. This is why I am here, to gain the right for the children, in law, to have a relationship with a father that loves them" was my opening statement.

They asked that the Cafcass representative be called in first as he had appointments in the afternoon. Both Lucy's solicitor and I agreed. He sat down and swore his oath. Lucy's solicitor began asking him questions whilst I took notes. It was my turn.

"Good morning, can you please tell me how much notice you gave Ms Jones that you were going to interview the children?" I asked him.

"I believe it was 48 hours" he responded. I knew already this gentleman was an honest man from our interview prior to court.

"Do you not believe that it is possible that the answers the children gave to the questions could have been scripted?" I asked him

"That is a possibility yes, but I don't think she did" he replied

"But it is a possibility? I just need a yes or no answer" I asked him

"Yes, it is" he answered. Lucy began shaking her head at me, realising she had declared war on the wrong person and I would go to any length within the law to win. Lucy was up next. I knew I was going to upset her with the questions I was going to ask, but there is nothing I wouldn't do to see my children.

Her solicitor began, he didn't ask many questions, just confirming her oath and confirming who she was

My turn. I took out the pack I had received from her solicitor, and turned to her statement. "Ms Jones, please can you confirm this is your statement?" I asked.

"Yes, it is" she responded.

"Is that your signature on it?" was my next question.

"Yes, it is" she confirmed.

"Also, can you confirm for us that everything you have written here is the truth? Bear in mind you are under oath" I asked.

"Yes, it is" she confirmed. At this point I knew I had her right where I wanted her. I glanced at her solicitor and by the look on his face he knew I was about to tear her to shreds.

"I would like to ask the court to go to page 1, paragraph 5 please" the magistrates all went to it.

"You have stated here, and I quote, Mr. Jones did not see his youngest son until he returned from Afghanistan. Please

A Father's Ruin

can you inform the court as well as me who was present at the Birth of Tom Jones?" I asked.

"He won't remember that" she replied.

"Ms Jones, that was not the question I asked, please answer the question, who was at the birth of Tom Jones?" I asked again.

"You were" she responded

"Please let the court note, she means me, Mr. Jones, the father of Tom Jones. Next I ask the court to turn to page 2 paragraph............."

"I ask the court where this is going" her solicitor jumped in

"Where are you going with this Mr. Jones" asked the magistrate.

"I am merely proving to the court that anything Ms. Jones states cannot be taken as truthful; she has already lied under oath and her statement has been proven as false" I cleverly responded.

"We understand and will take this into account Mr. Jones. Move on please" they asked.

"Will do. Ms. Jones, what is the reason you have to stop the children seeing their father on Christmas day?" I asked. She paused, went red in the face and her eyes began to water, I knew she had no good reason to prevent the children being with me on alternate Christmas days.

"It will disrupt their routine; they need to be at home on Christmas day" was her slow response. At this point I knew I had won alternate Christmas days, we had hours left to go and I was winning.

"Ms. Jones, can you tell me, do you have a temper?" I asked.

"NO" she said with a raised voice.

"Your worships, please can you ask Ms. Jones to calm down and not raise her voice" they did. Her solicitor was not impressed.

"Ms. Jones, is there any reason why you believe the children involved should only see their father on a Saturday day time instead of having a proper relationship with their father?" I knew the answer was because she wanted more money out of me, she would get more if this happened and I was hoping she would say it in court.

"Because they want to be at home with me" was her response. I knew the magistrates weren't stupid, they knew at this point there was absolutely no reason for this.

"Ms. Jones; You do realise that the father of the children, every other Friday drives all the way from Brighton, to Halifax, then to Birmingham, followed by the opposite on a Sunday, why can you not meet him half way every other Sunday to help ease pressure on both him and the children, also giving the children more time with their dad?" I asked

"Why should I? You chose to live in Birmingham; it's not my fault you're in Brighton". She replied. This could be interpreted as a fair answer, so I had to think quickly;

"So, what you're saying is, you don't care about the children's safety after long hours driving, and you are not willing to help to prevent danger to the children?" I asked, knowing this would both wind her up and show the magistrates that I was putting the children first, and she was thinking about herself.

"That's not the case at all" she responded "I don't see why I should drive anywhere for you"

A Father's Ruin

"No further questions" I said knowing she had just dug herself a great big hole, and she was stuck in it. It was at this point I knew I was going to get what I had asked for, I just had to cement it.

"Would you like to cross examine?" the magistrates asked the solicitor

"No more questions" he responded. I think he knew I had won already but he was being paid to do a job and was going to continue.

It was my turn on the stand; I swore my oath, stated my name for the record and allowed her solicitor to ask questions first. He asked about my financial situation, what I earned and my outgoings. I didn't lie, I told them everything. Then it was my turn to speak;

"For the record, I offered Lucy £1000 per month to ensure the children and she were ok. She chose to go through CSA. Yes I bought myself a new car, I earn my wage, and I work hard for my wage. I would like to ask that Lucy meets me half way between Birmingham and Halifax, and if it is money she is concerned about, I will pay for her fuel, I believe £20 per month should cover it. I don't think I am being unreasonable in what I think the children deserve. I believe the children deserve a full relationship with their father, and not a part time dad. I am a father, and I want to be a father, and I will continue to be a father to my children until the day I die, regardless of the decision from the court today. All I ask is that the court takes the decision from the children's needs, not from my needs or Lucy's needs. The only thing I am bothered about is the children, I miss them and I love them".

I was asked if there was anybody I wanted to call in;

"I would like to call in my father, Mr Tim Jones" I responded.

The magistrates allowed it so the legal secretary went to get him. He sat down and swore his oath. I looked at Lucy because she knew what was coming and she had a face like thunder.

"Mr. Jones can you confirm your name for me please?" I asked.

"Timothy Jones" he stated.

"Thank you, can you please tell the court how many children you have?"

"I have four men, they are no longer children, and they are now adults"

"Thank you, can you tell me, are you a single parent?" I asked, already knowing the answer.

"Yes, I am" he replied.

"No further questions" I told the magistrates. It was the solicitors turn to cross examine.

"Mr. Jones, why are you here today?" was his first question, I knew where this was going and it was only going to make the solicitor look bad.

"I am here for my Grandchildren. They deserve to see their father, he is a good dad, they have done nothing wrong to deserve this situation that they have unfortunately been dragged into, and I think it's disgusting that it has come this far" he replied, it was a reply I had to applaud silently.

"What makes you such an expert?" was the next question. It was the exact question I was hoping would be asked.

"I have raised four remarkable boys to become fantastic men. I believe being a father myself, raising my children to become the men they are today makes me more of an expert than yourself or any other person for that matter, especially as I am a single parent." His reply shook the solicitor;

"I'm sorry, this is a joke" The solicitor said, losing his temper. "No more questions". My turn again, this had gone exactly as I had planned it.

"Mr. Jones, is there any reason why these two children, in your personal opinion, should not see their father?" I asked. All three Magistrates turned and looked at my dad in anticipation of his reply;

Dad turned and looked at them;

"Harry is a good dad, who wants to see his children, he misses them. He is a good man and only wants to do right by the children. It's wrong to keep a father out of a child's life and I can do nothing but applaud any man who is willing to stand up and fight for the right to see their children. He is no angel, but who is, he works hard, and has done everything within his power and the law to get access to those children. There is no reason in my opinion why the children should not see their father" was his fantastic reply.

"No more questions your Worships".

"Mr. Jones, is there anything else you would like to add to this, for our benefit?" the Magistrate asked my dad, I did not expect this to happen, but I was extremely happy to go with it.

"Yes, Both Lucy and Harry have done wrong, it should never have come this far. They both should now allow for bygones to be bygones" he replied.

"Thank you Mr. Jones, we very much appreciate it, you may now step down". My dad then left the room.

"Mr. Jones, what exactly is it you are wanting to get out of this court today" they asked me.

"Well your Worships, I came today hoping that my children get what they deserve, a relationship with their father. I ask that they see me half of the school holidays; every other weekend and we alternate Christmases. This meaning, one of us has them from the 19th December till Boxing Day and the other from Boxing Day till New Year and swap the following year. I don't believe this to be unreasonable, and I believe it to be fair to the children. I also ask that Ms. Jones meets me at the services between Birmingham and Halifax to pick the children up. As I have stated I am willing to hand over fuel money, and again, in the interest of the children's safety, I don't believe I am being unreasonable." I stated.

"Thank you Mr. Jones," They then turned to the solicitor.

"Is there anything you want to add?" They asked him.

"No" was his response.

"We will now go to discuss this; we will meet back in this court room in 1 hour" they stood and walked out. I then walked out to go and get my dad when her solicitor called me over.

"Mr. Jones can I have a quick word?" He asked me.

"Certainly" I replied

"Don't worry, Lucy has left now, she has had to shoot off, I will call her after this with the decision the courts have made. I am going to say this off the record, I apologise for what went on in there." He told me.

"Listen, I understand, your paid to do a job, and you did it, it's no hard feelings."

"Thank you", he said, "Between you and I, she needs to grow up, I have been doing this job for 30 years, and to this day, I cannot do what you did in that court room. I applaud you, have you ever thought of becoming a solicitor?" he asked me.

I chuckled to myself as I said "I would love too, but don't have the time or finances to do so".

"Think about it" he said.

"Ok I will" I said as I walked off to go and see my dad and Brother and go for a coffee. We walked to the local coffee place, it was late afternoon, grabbed a coffee and we tried not to talk about what had just happened. It was nice. We walked back and not long after arriving back in I was called back into the court room.

"We have taken into account everything that has been said today, it didn't take us long to come to a decision on what was best. Before we go into it we would like to state that we don't like it when it comes to a court to make the decisions for children, we believe it is the job of the parents to make the best decisions in regards to their children. For that matter we see no reason why Mr. Jones cannot have his children on alternate Christmases, we do not believe it will disrupt the routine of the children and believe this was a throw away comment. Further to that we applaud Mr. Jones on his generous offer to pay the fuel cost for Ms. Jones to come and collect her children half way between Birmingham and Halifax and we see this as being more than reasonable, therefore it will stand. The children do deserve a relationship with their father and we see no reason why they cannot stay with their father for half of the school holidays and alternate weekends starting with next weekend. The question is, how will you sort this arrangement out?"

"Well your worships, I am quite certain that Ms. Jones and myself can arrange this ourselves, as this will be set in stone and legally binding" I responded.

"I do hope so Mr. Jones. You will receive a copy of the order in the post within the coming weeks. Thank you." The Magistrates then stood up and walked out. I could not have been happier, the decision was made, I had won, but it wasn't about the winning, it was the fact that she could no longer prevent the children from seeing me. I shook the solicitor's hand as a gesture to show there were no hard feelings and I walked out of the court room with a smile beaming from ear to ear. I told my dad and brother what the decision was and they both congratulated me. That was it, decision was final.

Chapter 5

PAM

After court I drove my brother back to Birmingham, I then Drove to Pam's house where I was staying. After a coffee I drove my dad to the services where he was being picked up. I was exhausted; it had been a long and mentally draining day.

Once back at Pam's I told her everything that happened, she seemed very happy for me and impressed. We had a glass of wine to celebrate then went to bed. I didn't sleep again, every time I closed my eyes, I would see the same thing, I knew it wasn't right but I ignored it and just got on with it.

Pam was a heavy drinker, we would drink every night that we were together, this began to worry me slightly, but I actually thought it was helping with the nightmares I kept having. Some were about real events that had happened; some were not real events but involved the same people. I now realise that drinking does not, in any way help with these situations.

I was coming to the end of my posting in Brighton, my RCMO called me to let me know I was to return to my unit in Germany. I informed him that I could not return, I explained how I had a court order in place to see my children and it was impossible for me to do so from Germany. I asked if there was any other posting I could take, and told how I was willing to forget any future promotions in order to stay in the UK. I was very quickly shot down and told it wasn't going to happen and I will be returning to Germany. I was not happy. I walked into my commanders' office and explained the situation. He was a very understanding man and would help in any way possible if he could. He told me to relax, and that he will sort this out for me. At this time, I made the decision to sign off. I went to my computer and filled in the form to hand in my 12 months' notice to leave the Army.

The following day my RCMO called and asked why I had signed off, so I explained to him the many reasons, and that they were not willing to support me when I needed it, and that I am not willing to work in an organisation that won't help me after I have given many years of loyal service to the Regiment. The only thing he could say was that he was sorry I had made the decision and I would still be returning to Germany.

A few months later I was called in by my commander. I was given my appraisal which was fantastic, recommended for promotion, as well as hoping I change my decision to stay in the Army. I thanked him and asked him if there was any news on me not going to Germany. Unfortunately, at that time there wasn't. I had only a few weeks till I was due to go and I was on my summer leave as well as relocation leave at the end of that week.

A Father's Ruin

I went on leave; I had already moved my stuff into pam's house and we were quite comfortable and happy. Still, the drinking continued. Six weeks leave, some of which I had the boys for, we had a great time. Constantly outside doing things, I loved it. Inside I was extremely unhappy. I didn't tell anybody, I just bottled it up. My phone rang a week before I was due to fly out to Germany.

"Sergeant Jones?" A voice asked

"Yes Sir?" I responded with no idea who was talking.

"I am retired Major Ford and I am at the recruiting office in Bristol, I have a man on long term compassionate leave and I need a man to cover him. I understand you are leaving the Army; how would you like to finish up your time here? I have cleared it through the Commanding Officer who has cleared it through your regiment. Your Commander in Brighton was the one who suggested it."

"I would be delighted sir, thank you very much" I replied.

"Take an extra two weeks leave and we will see you down here then."

"Thank you Sir" I then immediately called my old commander in Brighton and thanked him for his help. This was a manager who looked after his men.

I called Pam and told her the good news. She didn't sound too happy with it, she seemed to be off with me, I was chuffed so I let it go. Two extra weeks on leave as well. I had my kit sent to Bristol, and felt relieved. Deep down though, my feelings were beginning to get numb, I could no longer feel happiness as I used too, I didn't feel joy as I used too. I had nobody to talk too. I was beginning to hate myself.

Drinking was becoming a common thing between Pam and I, I never realised it but she only seemed to like me when she was drunk. We were engaged and this was turning into a farce, and I didn't realise it.

I started in the Bristol office; I was going to be a civilian in six months. I cracked on with the work I had to do, and started off staying in a camp 90 minutes away from the office. I met a woman called Rabecca. We became friends, only chatting by text now and again, it was completely harmless.

I decided to move out of the accommodation and move into Pam's house, it took the same amount of time to drive the distance, plus I got to see her. She seemed to like this idea at first, but this was short lived. We began arguing, often.

Rabecca was talking to me, and I began to off load the problems I was having with Pam on her. She invited me over for coffee, and I accepted, lucky for me Pam had broken up with me again because not long after I entered the house for a coffee with Rabecca was she all over me. She led me up the stairs to her bedroom, pulled down my trousers and took me in her mouth. It was nice to be wanted. We chatted for a while then I went to pick my children up. We had a good weekend together and Pam was at her mum and dads, so we didn't see or speak to each other for the whole weekend.

I took the children back to their mum and headed home to Pam's house, she still wasn't home. I relaxed with a coffee and as I was about to take myself to bed, she arrived back. We talked and decided to carry on our relationship. I did inform Rabecca of this and she kindly thanked me for telling her, but we carried on texting and chatting.

A Father's Ruin

I was then offered door work as head doorman on a nightclub in Tamworth. I soon accepted this job as it was an extra few hundred pound a month in the bank. I didn't have long left in the Army and had to have something to go into.

I was invited to an interview to become the security supervisor at Jaguar Landrover in Birmingham. I passed the interview and they asked when I could start. I was starting in the January, the week after leaving the Army on my resettlement leave. I was getting paid until April, so things financially were looking good for me.

I started the job at 0500 on the Monday morning; I arrived and began to take a walk with one of the team leaders to have a look around the sight. I introduced myself to the guards and let them know that I was their manager, any problems they were to direct them to me. I went the night before without a drink so I was fresh for that morning. I was in a very good mood, I was to work from 0500 until1700 Monday to Friday, plus they allowed me to work over an hour on the weeks I was picking up my kids so I could leave early on the Friday.

The problems were getting worse at home, I still wasn't sleeping and I was drinking every night. Pam and I would go through at least two bottles of wine, and if we wanted more, I would drive to the petrol station and buy some. I should have realised at this point that I was in big trouble and urgently needed help, but I didn't. One night I was drinking with Pam, out of nowhere she punched me in the chin;

"Don't fucking patronise me" she said.

I stood up and asked "What the fuck was that for?"

"You're a cunt, don't fucking patronise me" she responded. I decided to take myself to bed. The following morning, I got myself up for work and went in, I never take my home life into work, so I just pretended, as always that I was ok and everything was great at home. On the doors, the guys knew something was up when I started staying behind after the shift to have a drink with them, they never asked though, so fair play to them.

I was working my day job, as well as doors every weekend, and I was bringing in a good wage. All of my money went on Pam and her lids as well as my own kids. I never spent a penny on myself. Most would say it's unfair, but it is how I am. I looked after everybody else before myself. I always have and I probably always will.

Rabecca and I were still in contact, chatting and having a giggle, no harm no foul. Maybe it was wrong of me to talk with someone, but I didn't see that I was harming anybody. The problem was, Pam wouldn't allow me to have female friends. According to her it was good that I was afraid to talk to people of the opposite sex, and I was, in case she thought I was doing wrong. I now know I was manipulated in to believing this, but she wasn't the only one. She had mostly male friends, which, for my own stupid reasons, I trusted her with. I now know she was up to no good all the time, my gut was telling me throughout the relationship that she was, but I chose not to believe it. Always follow your gut instincts.

Things became bad when she decided to start going through my phone, in front of me, and I let her. I thought it was no harm as I had done nothing wrong, but she still looked regardless. She was constantly on the phone, texting every night, her male friends. I turned my phone off so I wasn't disturbed, but it didn't make a difference, she preferred to talk to her friends than her own fiancé. I still didn't click. There was one night we were having amazing sex, we were both drunk, as usual, but it was amazing. From nowhere she decided to head but me on the bridge of my nose. I sat up;

"What the fuck was that for?" I asked.

"Because you're a cunt, you patronise me all the time" she replied.

"I'm sleeping on the sofa, goodnight" and I walked out of the bedroom and slept on the sofa. As per, I got up the next day and went to work as usual, I received a very apologetic text. For some reason, once again I forgave her. I knew we weren't going to work, but still I was blind. My head was a mess, I was over tired, I was extremely jumpy and always on the lookout. Was this my life from now on?

Two weeks later, I went to bed early as I was tired, she was up drinking with the neighbours. At about 2am she came in the bedroom and woke me up;

"Harry, I need to talk to you" she said

"What's up?" I said thinking it was urgent.

"I want you out of my house, I can't stand you, I can't stand you touching me" she told me.

"Ok, I will pack my stuff tomorrow and leave after work" I said without surprise. I had a feeling it was coming and I knew it was just a matter of time. I went to work the next day, and I text Rabecca to tell her the news. She kindly offered to put me up in her spare room, and I accepted the offer. After work I went to Pam's house, packed my stuff and left.

I arrived at Rabecca's house with all my belongings, and unloaded them into the spare room and sat down with Rabecca and her friend.

Pam kept on bothering me, for the next few weeks, she expected me to be at her beck and call but when I didn't, she turned nasty. She told me she couldn't afford to feed the kids, so I drove over, handed her some cash and left because the kids didn't need to suffer.

One evening, after work, I received a call from her. She told me there was something wrong with the kids; I dashed over there to find they were in bed, asleep. She was drunk, and wanted me there. I was fuming; I left and went back to Rebecca's house. Turns out Pam wanted me back, and when I said no, once again she turned nasty. It is a never-ending circle.

Eventually, I got the car I had bought for her returned, after she very quickly fell pregnant to another guy. This made me realise what a fool I had been. I have had absolutely no contact with her since, I hope to never have again.

I was grateful to Rebecca for taking me in. Two weeks after moving in she declared that she wanted more than a friendship with me, I was not interested. I told her I wasn't interested, and she seemed to accept it. It was a Saturday morning and my phone rang, I answered;

"Hello"

"Hello is this Harry?" Said the person on the other end.

"Who is speaking please?" I responded.

"It's John, your mate Paul has given me your number; he is leaving the company and has said you're the only person he trusts to take on his job". This was great, I was thinking of leaving my job and this landed in my lap.

"Great, I will accept, when would you like to interview me?" I asked

"Can we meet next Saturday, at 5, at the New Inn, and we will talk?" he asked me.

"Great, can you email me the details and I will meet you there?" I requested.

"Yes, I will see you then". I got off the phone and told Rabecca all about it. She offered to take me to my interview, which I accepted the offer. I thought she was being nice, but it was all a big plot, which will become apparent later on.

Chapter 6

RABECCA

I was working as an area manager for a security company. I was on the go constantly, working over 100 hours per week and getting very little wage in return for my efforts. Rabecca went and got her SIA licence to work as a door supervisor. I took her on and employed her, and she was quite good at the job. However, one day I employed another female door supervisor to work a task with me, and when I told Rabecca;

"You fucking wanker, you fucking arsehole" she yelled as she was hitting the dashboard of the van.

"I'm going to walk" I said and got out of the van mid traffic. I thought I was well within my rights to employ whom I wish as I was the manager, but this was just the beginning.

I was helping out at Rabecca's business in my spare time, and after the shouting and mind control over a few weeks I went to the store cupboard and I took a strong rope dog lead. At the back of the land was a wood, I walked up to the wood and went as far in as I could, I text my ex-wife;

"Hi, please tell the boys I love them, and I always will" was what I asked of her. I went to a tree, wrapped the lead around my neck and round a branch and dropped. SNAP, the branch broke. So, I tried again, only this time the branch bent so I was stood on the ground, I decided to have another go. Once again, the branch snapped. I took this as a sign, it obviously wasn't my time. I walked back down to the office and carried on with my day. The pressure was getting too much for me. I was being forced into positions I didn't want to be in, I hadn't slept for so long, I was day dreaming constantly about things from my past that had happened to me and I had no way out, so I had to try to get it to end somehow, and taking my own life was the only way I saw to do this.

The day was done and I got in the van with Rabecca, as we were driving, she continued to yell at me about what I had done. I actually thought I had done something bad, when realistically I had employed somebody, that's all I had done.

"Stop yelling", I said angrily "Do you know what I have done today?"

"No, what?" she replied

"I went up to the woods and I tried to hang myself" I told her straight as she began to cry.

"AT MY PLACE OF WORK" she yelled at me; my immediate thought was that she was a bit selfish with that comment.

"Yeah, and I want to do it again but get it right this time, and I will tell you why, I can't cope with life anymore. I can't do it, it's all too much"

We got home and talked a little while longer, I went to the shop and came back. That night once again I didn't sleep. The following day I was offered a Job by Rabecca as a manager for her business. I accepted the job thinking it was because of my management ability and qualifications, but now I believe it was so that she could keep an eye on me. A couple of weeks later, my dad and step mum came to visit, Rabecca and I had just got together. He was talking as he does and he knew something wasn't right.

"I believe you need to go and speak to someone; I've thought it since you came back from Iraq the first time, but you are a tough guy. You will see someone when you're ready to do so" he told me. I obviously disagreed telling everyone I was alright.

A week or two later I was in the shop part of the business for the day, I was flicking through social media when I spotted something about mental health. It was written by a solicitors' firm, so I sent them an email. Within minutes they called me, it was one of the partners;

"Hello is that Mr. Jones?"

"It is" I responded.

"Hi I'm David from the solicitor firm you have just emailed, I am calling to let you know your case is being passed on and one of our secretaries will be in touch very shortly. The other reason is because I read your email and want to make sure you are ok? I have been through exactly what you're going through and I want to suggest that you see your GP as soon as possible" he asked of me. After our phone call, for an unknown reason I called my doctors to make an appointment, I was in a week later.

"Rabecca, I have a doctors' appointment next week" I let her know.

"What for?" she asked

A Father's Ruin

"Because something isn't right and I want to get fixed" I told her

"Want me to come with you?" She asked. I told her it was personal and I would be revealing things I have revealed to nobody. "You can tell me" She told me. To this day I am glad I never told her.

A week later I went to the doctor. I sat in with him;

"Harry, what can I do for you today" he calmly and kindly asked

"Doctor, I feel like I'm stuck in a grey cloud and nothing seems to exist. I don't sleep because I have nightmares and I have nightmares throughout the day as well. I struggle to talk, and stutter my words, I struggle with loud bangs and I have constant visions in my head of things I saw and things that happened to me in Iraq, and I tried to hang myself to get rid of it all" I was blunt and to the point, but I felt I had so much more to get off my chest.

"Right, I need to stop you there, it sounds like Post Traumatic Stress Syndrome. I am no expert at this, so I will have to refer you. Whilst you wait for your appointment to come through, if you need anything at all don't hesitate to contact us here. I will be prescribing you some anti-depressants for the time being."

Turns out that not only that; I was suffering with depression at the same time. One thing I didn't want was pity, I just wanted help, I wanted to think straight and sort my head out.

"Doctor, I also have no feelings, at all towards anybody or anything. I feel no fear, no hate, no love, and I don't like or dislike anything. I am completely numb inside apart from the hatred for myself" I told him with the hope of an explanation for this lack of feeling.

"I am not going to pretend to be an expert on PTSD, but from my understanding it is perfectly normal to feel this way when you suffer the way you are. You have been through an awful lot and it will take its toll, bear with us and we will sort you out. It's not an overnight thing but it will happen." The doctor seemed to know what he was talking about.

I was warned by the doctor that it could take some time to get an appointment, however due to my service in the military I will be jumped to the front of the queue.

"If there is anything you need, or you just want to talk, please don't hesitate to contact me, or another doctor here at the surgery. If it's an emergency call 999 and there are a number of charities you can all for help. I would recommend you contact a military charity as they may have a better understanding of what you have been through. But please remember, you are not alone and we are here to help". He told me.

Believe it or not, just those few words from my doctor made me begin to trust him, I trusted nobody, I thought I was being judged by all who knew me.

I walked out of the surgery with my prescription. I had two different types of tablets to take, one was to e taken once a day, the other was to be taken also once a day before bed o help me sleep, so I figured if I took them at the same time, I wouldn't forget the others later on.

I got home and straight away I got the twenty questions. "What did he say about us?" Rabecca asked. I got quite angry at the question.

"This has fuck all to do with 'us', it's my problem and I'm trying to fix it, any problems with us may be fixed as a result of it. But I don't appreciate you turning everything to being about us" I told her straight and thought she might back off. She did for a while.

I took my tablets that night, and very quickly found it was a huge mistake. I was quickly hallucinating, seeing two children sat on my draws, people were climbing out of my mirror, it was extremely discomforting. The biggest problem was the children I saw, more will become apparent later on.

Within a fortnight I received my appointment with the psychiatrist to chat with me and see how things were going. Between the appointments I had to get on with things and follow the advice of the doctor.

My appointment with the psychiatrist came around, I walked in and didn't trust the man in front of me. He straight away asked some very in-depth questions and made me feel very uncomfortable. "I find your case extremely interesting" he told me. This wound me up, I wasn't there for his interest, I was there for his help. He gave me a diagnosis of PTSD due to military service. Lucky for me, I had made an appointment to see my GP the following day.

I went the following day to see my GP and told him what happened, he told me to request a different doctor as he should never call your case interesting.

My next appointment with my psychiatrist was in two weeks. I received a letter confirming my appointment and luckily, I had changed who I was seeing.

The following appointment went a lot better; I was asked no in depth questions; I was only asked about how I was feeling and advised politely on how to improve my mood. I asked if taking up a sport would help, so I went to the gym and signed up for MMA.

A few weeks of doing MMA improved my mood, it seemed to be the only time I could get away from everything. No messages, no questions, just train, spa and fight. My temper improved due to this as did my personal fitness and my physical health. I got a few black eyes but it was worth it, at least until I got home. Questions would begin. I took up the sport for my own wellbeing and health, yet I was getting in trouble with Rabecca because she wanted to do everything with me. I was allowed no space at all, no freedom, nothing.

I now and again over the next few weeks would receive messages from my friends, some of whom were female. Rabecca took it upon herself to go through my phone; I was yelled at, and screamed at for messaging females. She had me remove my lock off my phone, giving her the ability to go through it whenever she wanted. This really dragged me down, the fact that I wasn't allowed friends unless they were her friends or approved by Rabecca. I knew deep down that what she was doing was wrong, but I could barely think straight let alone put up an argument to tell her she was wrong, so I went with it.

I received my first appointment for therapy with my psychologist, to go through cognitive behavioural therapy (CBT). I was not looking forward to this, another stranger wanting to know my life story, but I knew it was for the greater good. The appointment came around quite quickly; I went to his office and sat down. My guard was up; I didn't want to tell this man anything about my life;

"Harry, I am here for your benefit, you don't have to talk to me, and you can sit there in silence if you wish. If you want to just chat about the football we will do so, it's your choice. I wouldn't expect you to open up to me at least until you trust me, and I would like to build that trust before we begin the CBT if that's ok with you?" he explained.

"Sounds good to me" I told him.

"So, how are you?" I was asked

"Tired, constantly tired" I told him

"Is that due to lack of sleep?" he asked, but I got the feeling it wasn't to gather information, but as a general concern for my welfare.

"Well, the nightmares don't help, I don't want to fall asleep." Short and sweet I thought. I then expected to be asked about my nightmares, however, I wasn't.

"What do you want to achieve from this? How can I help you?" He asked. I thought it was a good question. For the first time I actually felt in control.

"I'd like the nightmares to stop, I'd like the day dreams to stop, I'd like the suicidal thoughts to go away and I want to smile which I can't remember the last time I did, and I have absolutely no sex drive." I didn't expect all of that to come out, but at least he knows.

"I will do my best to help you achieve this. The last thing to go will be the nightmares, they may never go, but you will be able to handle them better." He informed me. I was optimistic.

The appointment was short, due to me being uncomfortable. I made an appointment for two weeks later and I drove home, said hi to Rabecca as I walked in. "how did it go?" she asked.

"Not bad" I responded, thinking she would be understanding and not go in depth.

"So, what did he say about us?" she asked.

"For fucks sake, why does everything have to be about us or you? Why can I not have anything private? Why can't I discuss things confidentially with my therapist?" I was fuming, how dare she actually believe that I went there to talk about her.

Throughout the following couple of weeks, I was fuming. Every now and again little comments would be thrown my way. The worst thing she asked me to do was ask my therapist if she could come along. She had to have her way; I couldn't even have therapy on my own.

I made the mistake of agreeing to this. So I went to my appointment and I asked.

"I will not speak with her if you don't wish for it to happen, should you choose to let her come, she will only be told what you want me to tell her" he told me.

So, this was how I could test his trustworthiness. I will bring her along; she won't be able to help but rub it in my face if she got any information from him;

"Yeah, I think it's a good idea, if anything it'll get her off my back for a while" I told him, I also told him I wanted no information to be told to her. We moved on with the appointment.

"So, Harry, how's your sleep?" I was asked.

"What sleep?" was my response.

"How much have you had?" he was inquisitive.

"I would estimate I had about twenty hours in the last two weeks" I told him. He gave me some tips to try to help me sleep, which seemed positive.

A Father's Ruin

"What is it about the nightmares? Are they real events or fictional?" he asked. I could see no harm in answering honestly.

"To be honest, some are real, some are fictional and some I'm unsure about" I explained.

"How long have they boon going on?" he asked.

"You might think this daft, but it's been happening since I returned from my first tour of Iraq" I told him.

"Ok, let's talk about your tours" he said. I didn't like this idea, and I told him I didn't want too. "I mean so I know what tours you did and when, you don't have to go into depth with it" he explained. This put me at ease again.

"Oh, ok, well I was in Kosovo 2001 to 2002, my first tour of Iraq was 2003 to 2004, my second tour of Iraq was in 2008 and my tour of Afghanistan was in 2011 to 2012" I told him.

"Wow, that's quite a long time to have these issues spinning round in your head. Have they worsened?" he asked. I was unsure what he meant by this, so I guessed and luckily was right.

"The nightmares got worse with every tour I did" I briefly let him know. "So has my fear of fireworks, bonfire night is an absolute nightmare for me" I threw in there.

"How do you cope with that?" He calmly asked.

"Well I put the TV on loud, I close all curtains and windows and put noise reducing headphones on. It works ok but I have to do what I can to remain calm and I do what I can to ignore it. Once they stop or slow down, I try to be alone and curl up in bed to get over my feelings about it" I explained. The doctor had a very understanding look on his face, this made me start to believe he actually understood, finally, somebody who had an understanding and was willing to listen and not judge me. I was now at ease with this man, just that look on his face made me believe that he knew my problems and actually wanted to help me.

The session was cut at this point, he didn't want to wind me up anymore I don't think. The next appointment was booked for two weeks later, he shook my hand and I left.

I was dreading going home, I knew what was going to happen. I wouldn't be able to unwind; I would receive a barrage of questions and wouldn't have the privacy I wanted let alone I believe I deserved. I wanted what I talk about to be between me and my therapist, but this wasn't allowed.

I got home half an hour later to the usual questions that I had worked myself up to expect.

"Listen, I won't talk to you or anybody else about what I discuss with my therapist. He has agreed to talk to you, and I already know you're going to ask him about me, but he will not tell you anything because I have asked him not to discuss anything that I discuss with him".

"Ok, I look forward to speaking with him" she calmly informed me.

I made a cup of tea and sat down in the lounge with the dog and tried to unwind. In all fairness, this time I was left alone, it was great; I felt the stress starting to leave me.

After a few days of arguing I had had enough;

"I'm going to see my dad; I want to stay for the night there and get away" I told her. I had to get out before I exploded. I had so much rage going through me. The arguments were ridiculous and it wasn't me starting them. I had no sex drive and she couldn't handle that and was accusing me of all sorts. We spent 24/7 together and still

I was accused of doing things that were impossible for me to do.

I left the house, jumped in the car and drove to see my dad and step mum. On my way down I called and I was asked no questions, I was just offered some dinner and a pint. Dad knew why, he understood.

I arrived; "Hello, just in time for dinner" dad said as he answered the door. We hugged, I said hello to my step mum and hugged her too. We sat down, we ate and I was left to my own thoughts. Once dinner was done dad went and quickly got changed and called a taxi. We jumped in and headed off to the pub.

"Son, what's the matter?" Dad asked me.

"I just had to get away dad, I'm sick of arguing to be honest. I am trying to get my head round a few things but I can't." I told him.

"Like what?" He asked, without being intrusive.

"Well, why should I have sex if I don't want too?" I threw it out there to see the reaction.

"You shouldn't son." He told me straight to the point.

"Well, I feel I have too to stop arguments. I have no private life, I am sick to death of spending 24/7 together, I'm not allowed to do anything on my own. I mean dad, I can't even take a shit without being questioned about where I am and what I'm doing." I was on a roll.

"I don't know what to tell you son, do you think you could be happy?" He asked me.

"Yeah, I think we could be if she backed off and let me have a life" I told him.

"Have you told her?" he asked me.

"I have, but I struggle to say things I mean them. Maybe I should try explaining it again."

"Maybe, you don't know till you try" He said.

We took a seat at a table and we had a few pints. We got a taxi home and went to our beds.

As I climbed into bed, I text Rabecca and explained we needed to talk when I get home, she agreed.

The next day I got up, had a few coffees and a bit of breakfast then drove home. I arrived to see Rabecca sat on the sofa, it looked like an intervention and I didn't like it.

She began with the questions asking what dad and I talked about, what he said to me, what I said to him, what step mum said. I was losing my temper, I came home in a good mood, and run straight into a wall of questions again.

It turned out she called my dad and began to ask him what we talked about. Thankfully, dad told her nothing and sternly informed her that what we discussed was between us and she will never know the conversation we had unless it came from me. The sad thing is, to this day she doesn't know what dad and I discussed, but every time she saw him and spoke to him, she asked about that night.

The following week I saw my therapist and Rabecca was with me. I walked into his office and he reassured me that whatever I have discussed with him stays between us. After a quick chat I went down stairs and Rabecca headed up the stairs into his office. What was discussed, I have no idea, and never will. I never asked, however, Rabecca did utilise this to her advantage in any arguments by telling me that my therapist said bad things about me in her chat with him. I never believed this as it was patient doctor confidentiality.

This was how I knew she was lying to me, not only about this but other things as well.

I went in once Rabecca had finished. I asked no questions as I believed what they discussed was none of my business. I sat down and felt reassured, although I had no idea what was said about me between them, I really didn't care.

"Harry, how are you?" He asked.

"Honestly, I'm tired, and I'm struggling to concentrate. I'm drifting into day-dreams a lot." I told him.

"What is it that sends you into day-dreams?" he asked me.

"It could be something somebody says, or something I see, it brings up memories and the next thing I know I'm being woken from a day dream. The strange thing is I'm there, it's all real to me and it's not a dream, do you know what I mean?" I asked him, thankfully he understood.

"Do you want to go into a little detail? You don't have to tell me everything but I am intrigued and I think it could help for you to get the day dreams and nightmares off your chest. In fact, what I think could help, if you agree, is to list the things that bother you, and we can go through them, what do you think?" He asked me.

"To be honest I actually think that is a good idea" I was feeling relaxed, he wanted to listen to my problems. He grabbed his pad and a pen.

"So let's start with the biggest thing that bothers you" he said calmly.

"Ok, the biggest thing was what happened on my first tour of Iraq. We were on patrol when part of our route was to cross a very busy road. I was driving the lead vehicle. My commander gave me the good to go so I drove across the road. I got to the other side when my commander shouted to stop. I stopped immediately when a small truck drove into the side of us. I was knocked unconscious, and my top cover broke his ribs. Once I was brought round, I climbed out of the vehicle, and that was when I saw what haunts me. A woman was on her knees screaming as the lifeless bodies of two children were carried off to be taken to hospital. I knew in the pit of my stomach they were dead. I did that, I killed those children. We were placed under investigation by the SIB, and when brought in for questioning I was placed under caution for the deaths of the children. The officer that questioned me blamed everything on me, luckily it was all recorded. She then blamed my commander and she did the talking telling me what happened. I felt to blame, but I wasn't going to take my commander down with me. Thankfully my troop stuck up for me, but the two RMP officers on the patrol with us did nothing to support me and they didn't state I wasn't to blame which didn't help me. I was lucky to have nothing more come of it, but I believe it was due to the questioning and how it was incorrectly done." I had a tear in my eye as I was describing this to him.

"So, you felt a lack of support as well, I feel bad as they let you down" he said supportively "Let's move on and come back to this later on."

"Ok, my second tour of Iraq, I was on stag (stand too armed guard) on sanger seven in camp Abu Naji in Alamara. I heard the bang of a mortar being fired and immediately I picked up the field telephone and the mortar alarm was sounded. Seconds later I heard the whistle. This meant it was heading my way and would either hit me or around me. There was a huge bang, dust, dirt and shrapnel flew all around me, it landed less than a meter in front of me. The guy on sanger six called through to inform the guard commander I was hit. I informed them I had no injuries. I was bleeding from my ears and had ringing in my ears but I cleared the blood and carried on with my duties." I was calm when telling him of this. "You may laugh or judge me now, but the only reason I believe I am alive is because I had a guardian Angel watching over me that day, I know I should have died."

"And what is wrong with that? If that's what brings you comfort, who the hell is anyone else to tell you otherwise?" He said sternly, I very much appreciated this comment, it made me begin to feel sane, as though I was normal.

"On that same tour we had what I have been told was the biggest rocket and mortar attack on British troops since WW2. We had over sixty rockets and mortars fired at us in one night, and they landed all over our accommodation. There were shrapnel holes in every room, some colleagues were lucky to be out on patrol as their room was destroyed. We had one casualty with a shrapnel wound to her leg. One of the guys was refusing through fear to get into cover and my troop corporal was pacing up and down muttering to himself. I took control of the situation and dragged the lad out of his bed and threw him on the ground. I told him to get his body armour and helmet on and my troop corporal got a quick slap. He got down into cover and thanked me after. I could have got into trouble but he was glad I did it. This is one of the main reasons I hate bonfire night" I told him straight.

"Were you scared?" He asked me.

"No, I don't feel fear and I fear nothing. I put everybody else's safety before my own."

"You're a brave man Harry" he told me.

"The final thing that bothers me is the eyes. In Afghanistan after a fire fight the police collected the dead for families to come and collect. The bodies were dumped outside the police station and there was one that bothered me. Seeing the dead has never bothered me before but this guy was staring into my soul, he was telling me it was my fault he was dead. That look will haunt me for the rest of my life." I told him.

"Ok Harry, lets break these down and put it all in order. Which bother you the most?" He asked me.

"The children, the death of the children bothers me. They were kids, they'd be near enough adults now living a life, possibly with families of their own if it wasn't for me." I was getting very stressed and agitated, and I think he knew it. My temper was beginning to show.

"Then what we will do is, we will begin to deal with this next week if you're happy to do so. Let's start getting you back on track Harry" he suggested.

"That sounds like a plan to me doctor, thank you" I said. We booked the appointment for the following week and I went and sat in my car for twenty minutes, just calming down. I was so angry, and tense. I wanted to hit somebody so had to take a condor moment and unwind.

I started the drive home and I drove slower than the speed limit. I stopped twice on the way home just to calm down. Everything was annoying me, and I didn't want to come home and take it out on Rabecca. The whole drive home we didn't speak, she could see the anger in my face.

A Father's Ruin

We got home and I had to be left alone to unwind and calm down. I made a cup of tea and went into the garden to just sit and relax. I found myself just sitting there for a while and then I went inside. I was asked no questions this time. I think she realised I would explode if I was asked anything.

That night I didn't sleep, not a wink. I couldn't wait for my next session; I think he was getting the anger out of me, so I could then move past it.

I had a week until my next session, it seemed like forever. So I carried on working, getting on with life. Rabecca and I continued to argue, only this time it was different; she kept telling me I couldn't blame my behaviour on PTSD, and that my therapist had said things to her about me. I knew this was a lie, it was things he was not allowed legally to tell her and she was incorrect in what she said as well. This did nothing but make me extremely angry, the only feeling I had inside me was anger.

I decided to do something sensible and took out some accident insurance. Included in the insurance was accidental death, in which my children would benefit if I was to die. Rabecca hated this;

"Why did you not take insurance out for me?" She yelled at me

"Oh, I'm sorry, I didn't realise it was my responsibility to get you insured, fucking hell I'm terrible" I said with sarcasm.

"Yeah, well, you could have asked" she shouted

"Why? Tell me, why should I? You're an adult, sort your own out" I yelled back.

"Who benefits from yours?" She said hopeful. I knew where this was going, and I knew she wouldn't like the answer.

"My mortgage gets paid off and the kids get what's left as well as my half of my house" I said.

"All you fucking care about is them kids" she yelled at me.

"Big mistake" I warned "Yes they are, and yes they come before you, me and anybody else on the planet as far as I'm concerned. If you don't like it, then you can fuck off and we're done." I told her straight. She went quiet as I stormed out, I think she may have realised that she overstepped the mark and that I would not be putting her first, my kids come first, regardless.

I went to my next appointment. At this appointment we began the CBT. My therapist began to slowly wave his finger in front of me whilst I talked. Throughout it he was asking me how I was feeling. I won't lie, it was extremely hard, I was angry and getting angrier because I was uncomfortable. I had to explain, repeatedly about the death of the two children, he pushed me until my anger began to disperse. I really didn't want to do it, but knew I had too. Towards the end of the session, he warned me it may get harder in the next session, but he gave me some relaxation exercises to do at home. He told me to just get away from the problem and have an hour alone and relax until your calm, then go back to the situation. I explained to him that when I get angry at home, I have somebody following me around, constantly. He said I must explain it to her so she understands.

I got home and tried to explain it to Rabecca.

"I could do it with you" she said. This was when I was dead certain I wasn't allowed to do anything on my own, we had to be joined at the hip.

"Fine, whatever" I said as I had literally given up. That evening I made the mistake of leaving my phone with Rabecca. She took it upon herself to go through it and she saw a picture of me with a friend from a night out around 2 years prior. She went berserk. I had known this friend, whose name I won't mention, for over 10 years;

"She's married, with 2 children. I've known her longer than you and I know her husband." I tried so hard to calmly explain.

"So what, you slept with her that night didn't you" she accused me.

"Firstly, no I did not, secondly, I didn't even know you then, thirdly its none of your fucking business anyway" I was getting angry. From that point on she decided to tell me who I could and couldn't be friends with. She went onto social media and contacted my female friends. It was creepy, weird, not how things were meant to be.

After sleeping on the sofa that night, she apologised in the morning, but it didn't stop the remarks throughout the day. That evening we went to bed;

"Can you stop going on at me" I asked

"It doesn't matter, I deleted the photo off your phone anyway" she told me.

"Who the fuck do you think you are? Who the fuck are you to tell me what memories I can and can't keep? Well?" I exploded. I was sick of it. I wanted to be myself but she was trying to control me.

"It's done now, nothing you can do about it." Unfortunately, she was right. I went and slept in the spare room. I didn't get much sleep, I was livid. She followed me in, yelling and screaming.

"Leave me alone please, I don't want to talk right now, I need to be left alone to calm down" I calmly said to her. She got right in my face, near enough nose to nose.

"What the fuck are you going to do about it? You want to hit me don't you?" She was shouting. She was trying to push me to be violent making her the victim and me the bad guy. It was never going to work; I never have and never will raise my hands to a woman. After trapping me in the room, trying to push me to hit her for at least thirty minutes she broke down.

"I didn't want this" she said softly

"You think I did, all you had to do was leave me alone and let me calm down but no, you wanted to push me to violence. If you were a bloke, you'd have no teeth left in your mouth, consider yourself lucky you're a woman." I told her with pure anger in my voice. "Now, get out of the room and leave me the fuck alone" I strongly insisted. She walked out and cried herself to sleep as I lay there wide awake and fuming all night.

My next appointment came around and we went into more detail. As he waved his finger in front of me and I was talking I found the stress and anger was leaving me much quicker, and it wasn't as intense. I couldn't understand how he had done it but whatever he was doing was working. At the end of the session I gave my therapist the bad news that I was moving to Halifax soon, within the coming weeks. He suggested we get a move on. We booked the next session and I went home.

Not a lot happened through the next week, I chose to ignore the remarks from Rabecca, and I deleted social media to make my life easier. I lost a lot of friends that week, but I wanted to keep the piece.

A Father's Ruin

The next session with my therapist went even better than the last. I was calming quicker; my anger wasn't as intense. I felt good at the end of the session;

"Harry, have you looked at things from a different point of view" he asked me.

"What other point of view is there? If I had of ignored my commander, those kids would still be alive today, so it was my fault" I explained.

"Well, you were a soldier, you followed orders. Could you see the vehicle approaching?" he asked me.

"No, but it's not the point" I said

"It is Harry, there was literally nothing, without being able to see the future, that you could have done. You did the right thing at that instant and you followed the command of your senior. You did nothing wrong". He explained it "I think you should go home and spend the next week thinking about it from this point of view, I think you will see everything differently should you believe what I have said." He explained but I was sceptical, I wasn't sure.

I went home and kept replaying everything he said to me, over and over. He was right.

I had an appointment that week with my GP, I wanted to get my sleep sorted out. I did a written test about how and when I could fall asleep and I scored pretty high. I was referred to the sleep clinic to be tested for sleep apnoea.

A week later I was at another appointment with my therapist, my spirits were extremely high after the last session. My therapist said how well I seemed and I explained how it was thanks to him and how he changed my way of viewing things. He talked a little more on it and asked me to call should I have any other issues. I shook his hand

and thanked him for everything he had done for me. I understood, thanks to him that these things weren't my doing, I was doing my job. I also understood that in time my fear of fireworks may or may not subside, but I will learn to live with it. I would honestly say that that man saved my life. It was from that point on I saw the brighter side to everything, there is always a way out of any dilemma and there was always somebody to talk too should I need it. I vowed from that point to not lose my temper again.

Chapter 7

MOVE TO HALIFAX

A week after my final session we moved. I had spoken to Lucy and she agreed with us moving into the house Lucy and I owned. We would be closer to the children and I could find work.

We moved in, but unfortunately the tenants I had living there had ruined the house. The kitchen was destroyed, along with other damages done to the house. I didn't let this anger me; I knew I could get the damages repaired and get a new kitchen.

We went and got new beds for the kids, and other bits. It was going well. The first weekend we had the boys over, they were excited that we lived five minutes from them. We took them to the park. At the park there are some small skate ramps, boys being boys they were running up and down them and climbing over them. They got dirty, but as I taught them, as long as they're having fun, I wasn't bothered, clothes are cleanable or replaceable.

"Tom, look at the state of you" Rabecca yelled in a very stern and harsh voice.

"Who do you think you're talking too like that?" I quickly responded "He's a five-year-old boy, he will get dirty, he's a kid and he's having fun playing"

"Have you seen him, he's filthy" she responded

"I don't care, he's a kid, you do not speak to my children like that, do you understand me?" I told her straight.

"Your kids?" She said questioning me

"Yeah my kids, try talking to them, not yelling at them" I told her, she wasn't happy with what I had said; we didn't speak till the kids had gone back to their mums that night. I didn't say anything to Lucy, I didn't want any more trouble than I already had. That night she decided to end it with me. This was the sixteenth time she had broken up with me and I had previously warned her that if it was to happen again, I wouldn't take her back.

That night she left with some of her stuff. She text and apologised, I told her to give me a few days to think on things, decide what I wanted, to put myself first for once. What a mistake this was. She left me for one day and then hammered me for days. She asked if she could come and get some more of her stuff, and I agreed to it. She came by that weekend and went on and on at me. When she left, I made a cup of coffee and sat in the garden. I was enjoying the peace and quiet and was going over everything in my head when everything dawned on me. I was being controlled, I lost my friends, the only friends I had were her friends, I could do nothing without her permission, even down to work. I couldn't see my family without her say so, I couldn't even message friends to see how they are without her losing her

A Father's Ruin

temper. I didn't need this negativity in my life, I didn't need this kind of abuse in my life. I got on the phone and told Rabecca my answer was no; I did not want her back. She couldn't even accept my one request to leave me alone for a few days to think on things.

"Can I come and get my stuff next week?" She asked me.

"Of course you can, I will let you know a day" I replied, I thought it was the best thing to do, I couldn't keep her stuff, it would be wrong of me. I had applied for a job and had an interview on the Thursday. I text Rabecca and told her to get her stuff Thursday afternoon whilst I was at an interview, and she agreed.

I got through the interview and was immediately offered a job starting Monday. I accepted there and then. I arrived home to find a completely empty house. There was nothing but a bed and the kids' beds in the house. I immediately messaged and asked her to send me my stuff back as it was wrong of her to take my stuff. She said she would, but never did.

I went and got a new phone contract and informed everybody of my new number. I reopened my social media accounts to find that abusive messages had been sent to some of my female friends. They understood after my explanation that it wasn't me. Not only that my family had been deleted, again, it wasn't me. Rabecca had done it. I called round family members to inform them it wasn't my doing; they knew it wasn't and sent me the horrendous disgusting messages they received from Rabecca. The accusations that were made about me were disgusting. Not only that she contacted Lucy, and told her some disgusting things about me that was false, but she believed them. "I will prove to you somehow that I am not lying, I swear I did none of what she says I have done" I promised.

My brother received a message informing him that I was hiring escorts. Never in my life and never will I hire an escort. Upon going to the bank, I found my card had been blocked, when I called it turns out that my bank details had been used to attempt to hire an escort. It was on two occasions this happened, luckily the bank realised this was fraudulent and cancelled my card on both occasions. I put two and two together and the sums were adding up, I was under attack for simply saying no to having her back. She realised she couldn't attack my bank balance so she attacked my children.

I was at work when my phone rang on my break;

"Hi Harry, thought I better let you know that Rabecca has called social services on you" Lucy kindly warned me

"What for?" I asked

"She has told them a bunch of lies and I have told them it was all spiteful and wasn't true, but if I was you I would contact them immediately" she suggested. I thanked her for telling them it wasn't true and thanked her for the warning.

I sent an email to social services and explained my situation and told them I was free the following morning. The following morning my phone rang;

"Hi Harry, it's Michelle from social services here" a polite lady said

"Hiya, is everything ok?" I responded

"Yes thanks, thank you for your email yesterday; it has answered our questions, would you like to hear what was said in the statement about you?" She asked me

"I would please" I asked

A Father's Ruin

"You use your charm to cover up your mental health issues, you neglect your children, have no washing or cooking facilities in your home and your abusive" she told me.

"Well, firstly my children come first, and I am most definitely not abusive. My mental health issues are sorted; I was diagnosed with PTSD and have had the therapy. I do need a new kitchen which I am sorting but I pay somebody to do my washing and I do cook for my kids" I told her.

"We thought this was the case and it is what your ex-wife has said, we will not be taking the investigation any further so don't worry about it. We have to investigate but we figured it was out of spite that this was done" She explained to me. I thanked her and told her I understood she has to follow these things up.

I contacted the police as this was getting beyond the joke, unfortunately the police couldn't do anything apart from talk to her. I thought this would be the end of it, but then Lucy received a message from a random number telling her how I was banned from driving and there were naked photos of me being sent round Halifax. She sent the message to me and this was my opportunity to prove I was telling the truth.

I called the number with no answer, so I text.

"Who is this?" I asked. The first mistake was in their response.

"I am a concerned mother, your sending naked pictures to my daughter" this person replied. This was my new number, yet they knew who I was.

"Really? That's funny, who is your daughter? And how am I sending these pictures?" I asked

"I have seen my daughters snap chat; I don't want you contacting her anymore" I was informed. I found this weird as anyone who has snap chat knows the messages disappear after a few seconds, plus I didn't have snap chat.

"That's fine by me, but there is only one problem, firstly, the only person with naked photos of me is my ex, secondly, I don't have snap chat, so you have made a mistake, if there are pictures of me they have come from Rabecca, and I will be contacting the police." I replied. I showed these messages to Lucy who very quickly responded to this person telling them never to contact her again and also did the same to Rabecca in caser this wasn't her. She finally believed what I was saying.

I called the police and they still couldn't do anything. I was being attacked big time and nothing could be done. I could feel myself slipping back into a depressed state, but I was determined not to let that happen.

I received a letter the next day from DVLA, I had been reported as having sleep apnoea by a third party, and my licence was revoked. I accepted this and I am sorting it through the hospital. But I wasn't impressed that they took some random persons word for it.

A few days later I received emails from the loan companies Rabecca had taken loans out with and she stopped payments, so they were chasing me to make the payments for her. The reason for this was that I had been her guarantor. Everything had failed in her attempts to ruin me, however this wouldn't. Due to this I have had to sought help through a debt management company. The weight has been lifted from my shoulders and I am on my way back up.

Chapter 8

ON THE RISE

I find myself working hard to get life back on track. I work as much as I can to earn money, my debts (which aren't mine) are being paid off, my repairs are on the go to my house and I actually feel happy for the first time in many years.

I have given myself aims and goals for the next few years, this gives me a focus, something to work towards. It helps to take my mind away from the negativity in my life. It has taken a long time; this goes over the last five years of my life.

I see my children more than what the court ordered, and my ex-wife and I are now friends. She has a boyfriend and I am happy she is happy. I now see a future ahead of me and I now have a life. I have friends, my family back and I only keep the people in my life worth keeping. I have found that those who bring negativity into my life aren't worth keeping in my life.

Right now, I am focussing on getting promoted at work, I plan to do this within the next six months. Once that is achieved, I will then make a new focus, which will probably be to save to buy a new car. Every time I achieve one of these goals it will bring me a sense of pride and achievement, boost morale, increase my happiness and show me that life is much better now.

Although my job is not the best job in the world, I enjoy it and I believe I can go far where I am. I have a reason to get out of bed, I enjoy going to work, and I enjoy doing overtime. I like my colleagues and I don't feel at all discouraged at work. I informed them of my diagnosis and they are all supportive and always ask if everything is ok, which now, it is.

My family have all commented that I am back. I am me again and, in all honesty, I feel like me again. I can laugh again, I am sarcastic again, I wind people up at work and bring morale in the workplace. People now enjoy my company again, and I am learning to enjoy socialising again.

As I move forward with my life, I now see every day as a blessing, a gift if you will. Although I work hard, once I have achieved a few goals I can then calm work down and start to enjoy more of life. This is my ultimate goal and I will achieve this within five years. To me this is what I call being on the rise. I have been rock bottom; I have literally felt life is not worth living and attempted to end it. I have lived nothing but negativity, lived through hell and mental abuse but I am still here. I got help and now I am finally happy again.

Chapter 9

THE FULL TRUTH

So, let's put things into perspective. I have been through my hell, yes, I'm not proud of some of the things I have been through and done but I have learned for these things to live with me, not me live with them.

Following my operational tours, I ruined my marriage, for which I apologised and explained it was my biggest regret. Unfortunately, it can't be repaired, but we are on good terms and I hope she is happy, I have accepted responsibility for this, and I have learned to live with it. Once I ruined my marriage, I went into a relationship which was physically abusive as well as mentally abusive. I was treated like scum and for some reason I stuck around. Once that relationship was ended, I then entered into another relationship which I was reluctant to go into. I attempted to end my life as I couldn't take things anymore, I hated life and thought the whole world was against me and nobody could understand. I was mentally abused again but this time to a much bigger degree. I was broken down and manipulated, I was manipulated into signing things for which I am now paying the price. I have been beaten, mistreated, brainwashed, heartbroken, and practically ruined, but it is all become positive in the end.

I have had my good name attacked and dragged through mud, I have had my family turned against me, I have had my children attacked and I have been left in financial ruin. All this was after my military service. In all fairness I had no help from the military after leaving, I employed a solicitor to take them to court, yet they still fought it. After a year I received a war pension and six thousand pounds for my hearing loss. Currently I am looking at how I can pursue them to do more to help veterans with PTSD. Even if it's an interview with a mental health specialist on leaving, this could potentially save a lot of lives and problems later on as well as money. Suggestions get made but people who have been there and been through it are rarely listened too, simply because they are mot in position of power, this will not stop me from putting ideas up the chain to see if anybody will listen and support our veterans.

In order for me to conquer all these issues I sourced help through my GP and from there everything has been heading up. My life has been a rollercoaster ride since leaving the forces and right now I am climbing the ladder to success. Admittedly, I'm not high on the ladder, but at least I am heading up. Everything is positive, I have found that any negative can be turned into a positive and I now believe everything happens for a reason. I have lost friends on operational tours (May they Rest In Peace), but I have also lost friends who have taken their own lives since leaving the forces (may they also Rest In Peace). These friends shouldn't have lost their lives so early, if they had of been offered the help they required they would still be with us today. Gone but Never Forgotten.

Chapter 10

HELP

At first, I was ashamed to admit that I needed help, but very soon I realised it isn't to be ashamed of, but it takes a much stronger, bigger person to hold their hands up and say "I need help". I am a man's man, who has never asked for help in my life, known as a tough guy, and a hard man, but now, I believe I am stronger than most. I have been through my hell, and I have come out the other end with a smile on my face.

Although I haven't listed them, I have stated some of the signs and symptoms to look out for. Here are some of the main ones:

- Avoidance – Avoiding reminders and/or talking about traumatic events
- Reliving events – Be it in nightmares or daydreams, they all appear real
- Hyper vigilance - Always looking for danger and alert, on guard

- Sudden anger/irritable – Can become extremely angry at the blink of an eye
- Lack of concentration
- Sleeplessness/insomnia
- Self-destructive behaviour
- Personality changes
- Feeling of guilt/shame or fear
- Lack of feelings i.e. love towards people and staying clear of relationships

I must admit, I suffered with the vast majority of these, and I still do, but I am conquering them slowly. I have my personality back, and my anger has calmed down. I no longer feel guilty, but I am working on the shame. My sleep is returning to normal, although I still sometimes get nightmares. I am no longer self-destructive and I hope to feel love again one day.

I have learned there are people who understand. Talk to the NHS first, they helped me, they were absolutely fantastic. Even if you're not the one suffering, they can still offer advice for you to help those suffering. Look at charity, Combat Stress do a fantastic job, and they are not the only charity out there. Once again, they can advise even if you are a loved one of those suffering.

Talk, just talk to somebody, it feels great once you're on a roll and you realise there are people who listen and understand. Even if you feel awkward talking, your GP will keep everything confidential, and will help you. It is now set in stone that when it comes to mental health, veterans are jumped to the top of the queue, and you will be helped as soon as possible. Once you start help, I assure you, life will then become better, not straight away but as time goes and you get more off your chest, you will begin to see a future. Once the weight is lifted off your shoulders, you will see hurdles as hurdles and nothing more, you will realise you can jump over these hurdles and they will not stop you.

I now ask that all of you, whether you are suffering or are a loved one of those suffering, to make that call, see your doctor or call for advice. Once that ball is rolling, I can promise life gets better.

For more information about PTSD and the symptoms please visit the NHS website, or Combat Stress website www.combatstress.org.uk. There is a vast amount of information and advice on here to be utilised. In all honesty, this is where I started before going to my GP. Although I couldn't see the signs, everybody else could. As a friend or loved one, don't be afraid to ask the person suffering to get help, it may save their life.

Remember, you are not alone, and it is good to talk.

Synopsis

A man who fought for his country left with invisible scars. His whole life went to ruins around him, everything in his path he destroyed without even realising it.

After ruining his marriage, he was subject to abuse both physically and mentally for trying to be himself from people who claimed to love him. Broken, ruined, with nowhere to turn, nobody to help or understand he makes a life changing decision but does this work, or does it lead him down the wrong path? The only way is up and the sky is the limit when you're at rock bottom abandoned by the military.

This true story highlights the effects of war on a person. It goes through the losses and battles fought every day by our veterans. More soldiers and veterans have committed suicide than we have lost in battle, far too higher number, and something must be done about this shocking truth. This book will highlight the signs and symptoms of PTSD and tells of the help out there.

CPSIA information can be obtained
at www.ICGtesting.com
Printed in the USA
BVHW071546290719
554566BV00007B/940/P

9 781728 389257